Health and My Body

Stop the Germs!

by Mari Schuh

raintree
a Capstone company — publishers for children

Raintree is an imprint of Capstone Global Library Limited, a company incorporated in England and Wales having its registered office at 264 Banbury Road, Oxford, OX2 7DY – Registered company number: 6695582

www.raintree.co.uk
myorders@raintree.co.uk

Edited by Michelle Parkin
Designed by Sarah Bennett
Original illustrations © Capstone Global Library Limited 2021
Picture research by Morgan Walters
Production by Laura Manthe
Originated by Capstone Global Library Ltd
Printed and bound in India

978 1 3982 0306 8 (hardback)
978 1 3982 0305 1 (paperback)

British Library Cataloguing in Publication Data
A full catalogue record for this book is available from the British Library.

Acknowledgements
iStockphoto: Vesnaandjic, 23; Shutterstock: A3pfamily, 7, 9, ACorona Borealis Studio, 10, Andrii Zastrozhnov, 4, atsurkan, 21, DeeMPhotography, top cover, didesign021, 22, Elizaveta Galitckaia, 17, FamVeld, bottom cover, graphic-line, bottom middle 29, Irina Strelnikova, bottom middle 28, Kleber Cordeiro, 8, Lucigerma, 13, mirjana ristic damjanovic, 27, Monkey Business Images, 12, 20, 26, Niwat singsamarn, top 29, photonova, design element throughout Pikul Noorod, 15, Rawpixel.com, 11, SpicyTruffel, top middle 28, Stephanie Frey, 19, tmcphotos, 5, Victor Brave, bottom 28, top middle 29, wavebreakmedia, 25, Wor Sang Jun, top 28, yusufdemirci, bottom 29

Contents

Bold words are in the glossary.

Germs and you

Look around. Can you see any germs? Check on the table. You can't see germs there. Look at your hands. Nothing there either. No matter how hard you try, you can't see germs. But they are all around us.

Germs under a microscope

Even if something looks clean, germs
can still be on it. Germs are tiny living
things. You need to use a **microscope**
to see germs.

Good germs

Germs are found in many places. But you don't have to be afraid of them. Being around germs can be a good thing. Your body learns how to fight off bad germs.

Some germs are helpful. One type of germ is called **bacteria**. Good bacteria lives in our bodies. This type of bacteria doesn't make us sick. It helps our bodies use the **nutrients** in the foods we eat.

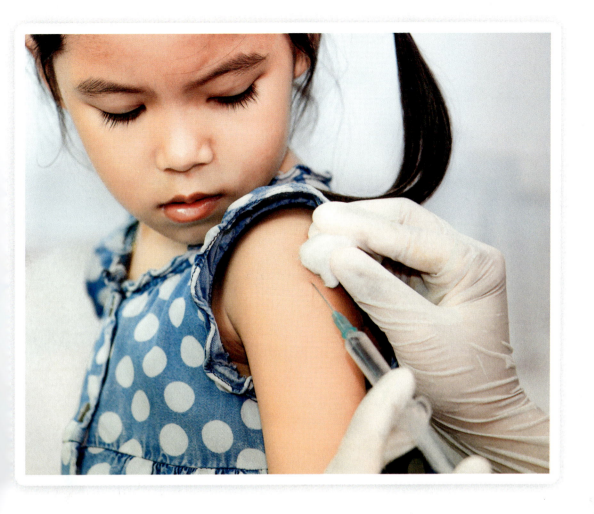

Doctors use some germs to make medicines. Germs are also used to make **vaccines**. Vaccines help prevent diseases. Some vaccines are given by injection. You might have had a flu vaccine by injection. You probably had vaccines as a baby.

Getting ill

Some germs can make you poorly.
You can get the flu. You can get a
cold. Germs can also cause **infections**.

There are many ways germs can get into your body. You can breathe in germs through your nose or mouth. Germs can be on your food. Germs can get in through a cut in your skin. If you rub your eyes with dirty fingers, germs can get in your eyes.

Coronavirus

Viruses are a type of tiny germ. They can make you feel poorly. A coronavirus is the type of virus that can give you a cold. It can also make people ill with more serious illnesses.

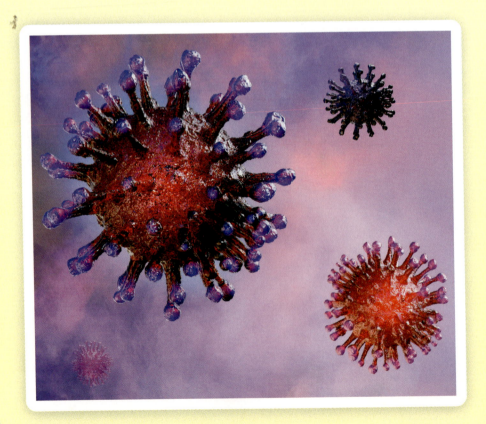

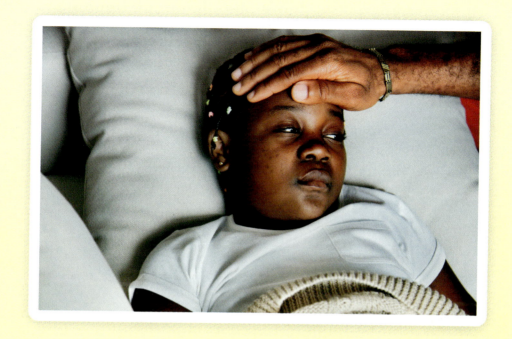

A new virus

In 2019, a new virus started spreading around the world. It is a new type of coronavirus. It causes the disease COVID-19. If a person is infected with this coronavirus, they may feel poorly. They may have a cough and feel hot. But our bodies are very good at fighting the virus. Nearly everyone who gets it will feel better after a few days.

Protecting people

Some people's bodies are not as strong as others. They may be old, or may already have an illness that makes their body weaker. Some of these people might struggle to fight off the new coronavirus. They may become more poorly and need help from doctors and nurses. They may even need to go to hospital.

Around the world, people are working together to protect those most at risk from the new coronavirus. To stop the virus spreading around too much, people stayed away from others for a while. Some shops were shut. Even schools were closed. Many people now wear face masks when they go out. All these things have helped to slow the virus down and keep us safe.

Washing your hands

There are lots of other ways to help stop the coronavirus and other germs from spreading. The best way is to wash your hands. Use warm water and soap. Then scrub, scrub, scrub! Clean between your fingers. Wash your wrists too. Clean under your fingernails.

Wash your hands for about 20 seconds. Don't rush. As you wash, sing the "Happy Birthday" song or say the alphabet twice. Then, rinse and dry your hands well. Germs can spread in wet places.

It's important to wash your hands through the day. Make sure you wash before and after you eat. Wash after you go to the toilet. Have you played outside or played with a pet? Wash your hands when you've finished.

What do you do if there is no sink nearby? Then you can use hand sanitiser. This is a special liquid. It does not wash off dirt. But it kills germs. Ask an adult to help you use it. Be sure the liquid covers your hands, fingers and wrists. Rub it in until it dries.

Staying healthy

People sneeze. They cough. Germs go into the air. Other people can breathe in the germs. The germs can make them ill.

You can help to keep germs out of the air. Cover your mouth when you cough. Sneeze into a tissue. Then wash your hands.

Can you feel a sneeze coming on? Oh, no, you've run out of tissues! Don't sneeze into your hands. Sneeze into your elbow.

Eating healthy foods helps your body to fight germs. Make sure you eat fruit and vegetables. Try new foods! Eating different healthy foods helps you get the nutrients your body needs. Drink lots of water every day.

Get moving to keep your body strong. Be active every day. Play outside. Run around or ride your bike.

Your doctor can help you to stay healthy. A nurse can give you vaccines against flu and other diseases. Injections might hurt a little bit. But they are important. They keep your body strong. They can get your body ready to fight off germs and diseases.

What should you do if you get ill?
Tell a parent if you don't feel well. He
or she may see if you have a **fever**. You
may have to stay at home from school
or visit the doctor. Get lots of sleep.
Drink lots of water. Try not to touch
your eyes, mouth or nose. This will all
help you to get better.

Keeping clean

Stay clean to keep germs away. Germs can get on your fingers. Try not to bite your fingernails. The germs could get inside your mouth. Yuck! Ask a parent to trim your fingernails instead.

Dirty, smelly clothes can have germs on them too. Try to wear clean clothes. Keep your bedroom clean of old dishes and plates. Put them in the kitchen, ready to be washed. A clean house has fewer germs.

Germs at school

Your school is a busy place. There are lots of people inside. You can get ill from others at school. It's not a good idea to share items, such as water bottles and lip balm. This can spread germs. Don't use the same spoons, forks or cups.

Do you have a backpack? Clean it out when you get home. Use a cloth to wipe out the inside. Clean the outside too. When you get to school, hang up your backpack. Don't put it on the floor. Floors can be dirty.

Help stop germs!

Wash your hands
Soap kills germs. Wash your hands carefully several times a day. If you can't use soap and water, use hand sanitiser.

Use a tissue
If you need to wipe your nose, use a tissue then put it straight in the bin.

Use your elbow
If you cough or sneeze, do it into your elbow, not your hand.

Keep clean

Wash your body and your hair and keep clean.

Keep your things clean

Use clean water bottles, plates and cutlery. Don't share these things with others.

Eat well

Eat healthy foods to keep your body working well.

Keep fit

Exercise every day to keep your body strong.

Rest

If you are ill, rest as much as you can. You'll soon feel better!

29

Glossary

bacteria very small living things that exist all around you and inside you

fever a rise in body temperature, sometimes it means you are poorly

infection an illness or disease caused by germs

microscope a tool that makes very small things look large enough to be seen

nutrient part of food, like vitamins, that our bodies use to grow and stay healthy

vaccine medicine that prevents a person from getting a disease

virus tiny germs that can cause illness

Find out more

Coronavirus A book for Children, Elizabeth Jenner, Kate Wilson and Nia Roberts (Nosy Crow, 2020)

Germs, Lisa Cline-Ramsome (Henry Hold and Company, 2017)

The Bacteria Book. Steve Mould (DK/Penguin Random House, 2018)

Websites

What germs can be found on your hands?
www.bbc.co.uk/bitesize/clips/zmcg9j6

What are germs?
kidshealth.org/en/kids/germs.html?WT.ac=p-ra

Why do I need to wash my hands?
kidshealth.org/en/kids/wash-hands.html?WT.ac=k-ra

Index